Cigarettes

Cigarettes

Elaine Landau

Watts LIBRARY™

Franklin Watts
A Division of Scholastic Inc.
New York • Toronto • London • Auckland • Sydney
Mexico City • New Delhi • Hong Kong
Danbury, Connecticut

For Michael

Note to readers: Definitions for words in **bold** can be found in the Glossary at the back of this book.

Photographs © 2003: AP/Wide World Photos: 36 (David Duprey), 23 (Mickey Krakowski); Art Resource, NY/Smithsonian Amercian Art Museum: 6; Corbis Images: 21 (Lester V. Bergman), 13 (Bettmann), 2 (Farrell Grehan), 11 (Hulton-Deutsch Collection), 38 (Reuters NewMedia Inc.), 14 (The Purcell Team); Custom Medical Stock Photo: 5 left, 25, 26; Fundamental Photos, New York/Richard Megna: cover; Getty Images: 48 (Ken Lambert/Liaison), 50 (Alex Wong/Newsmakers); Photo Researchers, NY: 9 (Frederica Georgia), 46 (Jeff Greenberg), 15 (Bill Aron); PhotoEdit: 5 right, 43 (Billy E. Barnes), 28 (Myrleen Cate), 41 (Susan Van Etten), 34 (Tony Freeman), 18, 32, 44 (Michael Newman), 22 (Novastock), 30, 37 (David Young-Wolff); The Image Works/Bob Daemmrich: 16, 17.

The photograph on the cover shows a cigarette burning in an ashtray. The photograph opposite the title page shows a woman working at a cigarette factory.

Library of Congress Cataloging-in-Publication Data

Landau, Elaine.
    Cigarettes / by Elaine Landau
    p. cm. — (Watts library)
    Summary: Discusses the health issues associated with smoking, history of tobacco use in the United States, and the various ways to quit smoking.
    Includes bibliographical references and index.
    ISBN 0-531-12024-4 (lib. bdg.)   0-531-16666-X (pbk.)
    1. Cigarette habit—United States—Juvenile literature. 2. Tobacco habit—United States—Juvenile literature. [1. Smoking. 2. Cigarette habit. 3. Tobacco habit.] I. Title. II. Series.
HV5760 .L35 2003
613.85—dc21   2002006151

Contents

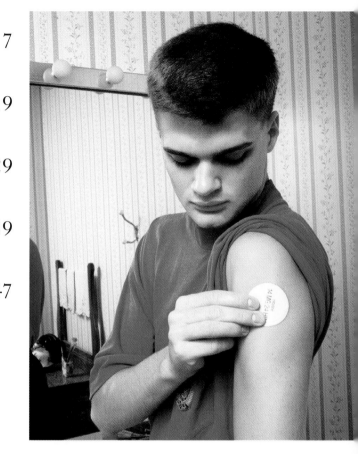

Tobacco has long played a role in American Indian ceremonies. Today, however, the group Native Americans Stopping Tobacco in Youth holds powwows to discourage young people from smoking.

Chapter One

History of Tobacco

There is nothing new about smoking tobacco. People have done it for centuries. Before Europeans ever set foot in the Americas, native peoples in the region used tobacco. Sometimes they smoked it in pipes. In tropical areas, people wrapped large tobacco leaves around smaller ones, creating the first cigars.

American Indians smoked for pleasure and also used tobacco in a variety of ceremonies. Some were religious rituals. Other ceremonies were performed for healing purposes. At times tobacco was used to dress wounds. It was also believed to be a painkiller.

Tobacco Crosses the Atlantic

Columbus was among the first explorers to bring tobacco back to Europe. Over the next century, tobacco would be introduced in many parts of the world. Dutch and Portuguese explorers brought it to China, Japan, Turkey, and the East Indies. Along with coffee, sugarcane, and chocolate—tobacco became one of the treasures from the Americas.

In Europe, the supposed healing powers of tobacco were frequently praised. Tobacco was said to ward off the plague, act as a laxative, and improve memory. There were also claims that it cured **melancholia**, or what today is known as depression. Yet even back then, tobacco had its opponents. Through the years, many spoke out against smoking. They described it as an ungodly and disgusting habit. Nevertheless, the growing fascination with tobacco caused people to try it. Once they did, they were soon hooked on this habit-forming substance.

Much of the demand for tobacco in England and other European nations would initially be met by the southern colonies. In the 1600s tobacco was grown in the Jamestown Colony of Virginia. Before long, it would be cultivated throughout the area. As plantations sprang up throughout the South, the population there came to depend heavily on tobacco for its livelihood. A great deal of labor was needed to

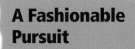

A Fashionable Pursuit

The trendsetting English explorer Sir Walter Raleigh loved to smoke. Raleigh helped make smoking popular in high society circles.

This photograph shows how a tobacco field might have looked in colonial times.

An Impressive Plant

A tobacco plant can grow as high as 9 feet (3 meters). Its arrow-shaped leaves are about 18 inches (46 centimeters) long.

grow and harvest this crop. This proved to be a factor in the ongoing African slave trade.

Although tobacco was exported to other countries and even grown elsewhere, by the 1800s Americans were the world's most ardent tobacco users. They grew it, sold it, and smoked it. This was especially true in the South, where tobacco had become an important part of many people's lives.

Cigars, Cigarettes, or Snuff

There were many ways people used the exceedingly popular tobacco plant. Some chewed tobacco. Others smoked it in pipes or wrapped in its leaves as a cigar. In fashionable European circles it became popular for people to place a form of tobacco, known as snuff, in their noses.

In the United States, cigarettes made a significant debut during the Civil War. At the time, cigarettes were even packed into both Rebel and Union soldiers' food rations as a special treat. These were small cigarettes that could be quickly smoked before battle or while on the move. For some Northern soldiers, it was their first taste of tobacco.

Snuff was another tobacco product used in the United States. While it was largely inhaled by the British, Americans preferred to place a pinch of snuff between their cheek and gum. Women who used snuff usually did so differently, however. They would dip a small hickory stick moistened with salvia into the snuff container and then suck on the stick.

Women who smoked cigarettes often had to do so in

secret. Smoking was seen as unseemly for "the fairer sex." Some areas even passed laws prohibiting women from smoking in public. In 1904, a woman smoking a cigarette while riding in a car in New York City was arrested. The police officer taking her into custody had pulled the cigarette from her hand and angrily informed her, "You can't do that on Fifth Avenue!" Female schoolteachers caught smoking—even those who did so while hiding in the school supply closet—were often promptly dismissed as well.

In the early 1900s, it was considered improper for women to smoke cigarettes.

11

Until the years just preceding World War I, cigarette smoking remained on a fairly even keel. But just as troops received cigarettes during the Civil War, throughout World War I they were shipped overseas to American soldiers fighting in Europe. Cigarettes were seen as a powerful morale booster, and millions were distributed free of charge to U.S. soldiers. Soldiers were not the only ones smoking. Even before the war, cigarettes had begun to catch on across the United States. Prior to 1910 less than 10 billion cigarettes were smoked annually. By 1919 nearly 70 billion cigarettes a year were produced. That was an increase of more than 600 percent. The habit was becoming increasingly common among large numbers of Americans.

Medical Consequences

Doctors were among the first to notice the consequences of the cigarette trend. Lung cancer had previously been an extremely rare disease in the United States but this was beginning to change. By the 1930s the medical profession was looking for new ways to deal with the rash of cases that had begun to appear.

Some wondered if cigarettes could have been the cause of the increase in lung cancer. Yet despite these suspicions, there was still no proof that cigarettes were harmful. In fact, the tobacco industry had launched an extensive advertising campaign implying the opposite. Cigarette manufacturers wanted the public to believe that cigarette smoking actually had some

A New Epidemic

Dr. Alton Ochsner was a leader in exposing the hazards of tobacco and its link to cancer. As a medical student, Ochsner had seen what was considered a rare occurrence—a patient with lung cancer. He later wrote, "I did not see another case until 1936, seventeen years later, when in a period of six months, I saw eight patients with cancer of the lung. Having been impressed with the extreme rarity of this condition . . . this represented an epidemic for which there had to be a cause. All the afflicted patients were men who had smoked since World War I . . . . I had. . . at that time [reasoned] that the probably cause of this epidemic was cigarette use."

health benefits. One 1930 ad for the cigarette brand Lucky Strikes claimed that 11,105 doctors believed that Lucky Strikes were "less irritating to sensitive or tender throats than any other cigarette."

This advertisement used an athlete to promote Lucky Strike cigarettes. Notice the phrase, "Cream of the Crop." Does that refer to the athlete, the cigarettes, or both?

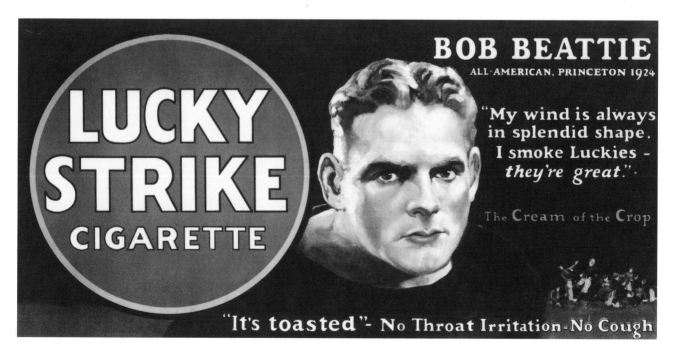

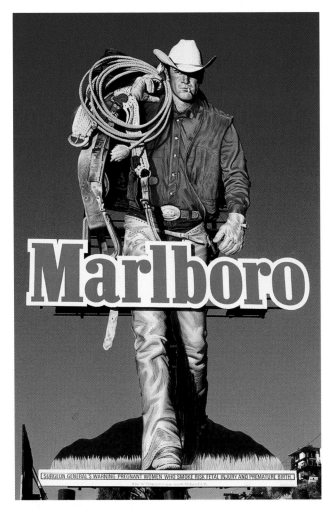

One of the most internationally known cigarette advertising campaigns used the image of the cowboy to entice people to buy the product.

However, these claims could not stand up in the face of mounting evidence showing cigarettes in a less favorable light. As early as 1932, a paper published in the *America Journal of Cancer* accurately identified the tars in cigarettes as causing cancer. In 1950, the first article linking smoking to lung cancer was published in the *Journal of the American Medical Association*. By the mid-1950s other studies were connecting cigarettes with a number of serious health concerns.

While the health benefits of cigarettes were in question, the tobacco companies continued to lure people to use their products by portraying smokers as attractive, chic, and even intelligent. Cigarette manufacturers spent millions sponsoring television shows whose stars smoked at every turn. Television commercials and billboard advertisements took the same approach. An ad for Marlboro cigarettes showed a lone cowboy on horseback with a cigarette in his mouth. It tried to tie ruggedness, strength, and masculinity to the

Marlboro brand. Years later one of the actors who played the Marlboro man died of lung cancer.

Officially Condemned

The first official condemnation of smoking in the United States came in January 1964 in a document known as the "1964 Surgeon General's Report on Smoking and Health." The report cited smoking as a major cause of lung cancer. It also linked smoking to numerous other forms of chronic lung disease.

By January 1966, the Federal Trade Commission required cigarette packaging and advertising to carry the warning: "Caution: Cigarette Smoking May Be Hazardous to Your Health." Further measures were taken in 1970 when Congress passed the Public Health Smoking Act. This legislation required stronger warnings on both cigarette packaging and printed cigarette advertisements. Cigarette commercials were also no longer permitted on either television or radio.

SURGEON GENERAL'S WARNING: Smoking By Pregnant Women May Result in Fetal Injury, Premature Birth, And Low Birth Weight.

The first warnings about the dangers of smoking appeared on cigarette packages and advertisements in the late 1960s.

Texas students carried crosses to their state capital. The crosses symbolized the number of people who die every day as the result of smoking.

Aware of possible problems ahead, cigarette manufacturers worked on ways to counter negative publicity. This resulted in the manufacture of numerous low-tar, low-**nicotine** filtered cigarettes. These light cigarettes held out a tantalizing promise. Smokers would supposedly be able to enjoy cigarettes without jeopardizing their health.

Low-tar and low-nicotine cigarettes proved not to be the

answer after all. Although the nicotine and tar in cigarettes can be lessened, the same is not true for the **carbon monoxide** they produce. Studies also showed that smokers who switched to light brands tended to smoke more cigarettes and draw in more tar and nicotine with each puff.

Since the 1980s cigarettes have been attacked by doctors, lawyers, politicians, and community groups. There have been lawsuits and legislation designed to curb smoking. Yet people continue to smoke. This occurs even though about 430,700 Americans die each year because of cigarettes.

Serious Evidence

More than 40,000 medical studies have connected cigarette smoking to disease and death.

Kids and smoking are a dangerous combination. Many young people may not realize how addictive cigarettes can become. Tobacco companies have tried to make young people smokers by manufacturing honey- and cola-flavored cigarettes.

Chapter Two

Physical Effects of Cigarettes

Picture a person on drugs. You probably did not think of a smoker. Yet tobacco contains a very powerful **addictive** drug known as nicotine. Nicotine is a colorless liquid found in the tobacco plant's leaves. Nicotine is one of more than 4,000 chemicals found in cigarette smoke. When you smoke, you inhale a mixture of chemicals and gases that contains

A Dubious Distinction

Nicotine was named for Jean Nicot de Villemain. He was a sixteenth-century French ambassador to Portugal who sent a tobacco sample to the French royal court.

nicotine. This mixture sweeps across your lips, through your mouth and down into your lungs. There it mixes with oxygen and is rapidly absorbed into the bloodstream, which carries it throughout the body.

The nicotine in cigarette smoke is fast acting. It affects the brain within seven seconds. Nicotine acts the way other drugs, such as cocaine and amphetamines do, but to a lesser extent. It affects a part of the brain believed to be responsible for drug-induced pleasurable feelings. Over time this leads to addiction. Nicotine produces other effects as well. It increases mental alertness. It also increases heart rate and blood pressure and restricts blood flow to the heart muscle.

Smokers like how nicotine makes them feel, but it is hardly a harmless substance. In high concentrations, nicotine is extremely deadly. A single drop of purified nicotine on your tongue can kill you. Because of its **lethal** qualities, nicotine has been used as a **pesticide** for hundreds of years.

Health Risks

Cigarette smoking can result in some very serious illnesses. Perhaps the best-known health risk associated with smoking is cancer. Forty-three chemicals found in cigarette smoke are now known to cause cancer. Not surprisingly, about 90 percent of all lung cancer cases have been linked to cigarettes. Lung cancer is the number one cause of cancer-related deaths in both men and women. Cigarettes can also cause other cancers. They have been linked to cancer of the

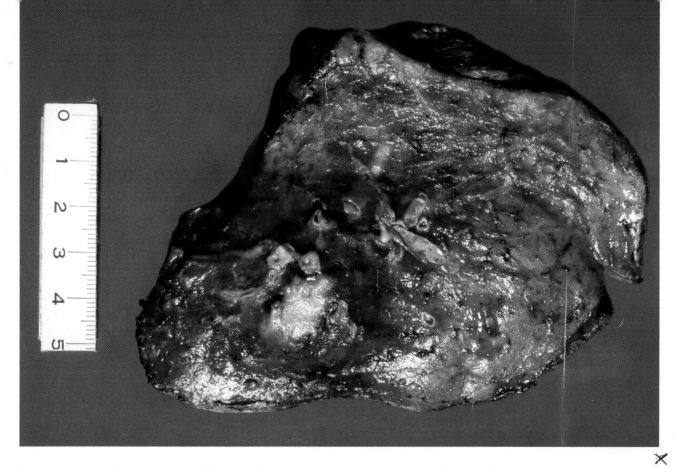

This photograph shows a lung that was removed because of lung cancer.

larynx, esophagus, bladder, kidney, pancreas, stomach, and other organs.

Smoking also causes some serious **respiratory** diseases. These include **emphysema**—an illness that robs a person of his or her ability to breathe. Many smokers develop emphysema. It happened to Mickey, a middle-aged man who started smoking as a teen. Mickey described what things were like for him at this point in his life:

"Because of emphysema, my wife will never have the good husband that she deserves and my daughter will never have the father that other children have, and this tears my heart out. What a lot of people do not realize is that emphysema is

Smoking causes a number of respiratory diseases, including emphysema and chronic bronchitis.

terminal . . . it kills you. The problem is that it is very sneaky and it destroys a little bit of your lungs at a time so you don't even realize that there is a problem until it is too late."

Mickey posted his story on an Internet site for smokers, hoping to encourage others to quit. He died later that day.

Smokers also frequently suffer from chronic bronchitis. In this case, the smoker may cough continually. In addition, cigarette smoke triggers asthma attacks in smokers and nonsmokers. Undoubtedly, smoking-related lung ailments take a serious toll on many people's lives.

Other organs, such as the heart, are affected by cigarette smoking as well. For smokers, the chance of developing heart disease is doubled. Smokers who have had heart attacks are more likely than non-smokers to have a second heart attack. Smoking cigarettes can even affect the blood vessels. It raises a person's chances of having a stroke.

Nowhere to Hide

No smoker, regardless of how important that person is or how much money he or she has, can avoid the pitfalls of this dangerous habit. Patrick Reynolds's grandfather founded the R. J. Reynolds Tobacco Company, which was among the world's largest tobacco corporations. Despite their financial success, the Reynolds family suffered the health consequences of using their own product. Patrick noted:

> *"My grandfather, R. J. Reynolds, chewed tobacco and died of cancer of the pancreas. My father smoked heavily and he died at fifty-eight after years of suffering from emphysema. My father's sister, Nancy, smoked and died of cancer. One of Nancy's children, my cousin, smoked, and died recently of cancer. My mother smoked, and I believe that smoking contributed to her death as well."*

Despite his family's experiences, Patrick began smoking himself. After years of trying to quit, he finally managed to

Patrick Reynolds talks to students about the dangers of smoking. Reynolds's father died of emphysema when Reynolds was only fifteen years old.

stop smoking. Afterward he dedicated a portion of his inheritance from his family's tobacco fortune to a "stop smoking" program.

Secondhand Smoke

You don't have to smoke to be harmed by cigarettes. Inhaling smoke from a nearby smoker's cigarette can hurt you. This smoke is called **secondhand smoke** or environmental tobacco smoke (ETS). Inhaling it is called **passive smoking**.

Secondhand smoke contains even more harmful chemicals than smokers are exposed to. That's because secondhand smoke is made up of 80 percent **sidestream smoke** and 20 percent **mainstream smoke**. Sidestream smoke is the smoke from the lit end of a cigarette that never passes through the filter. It flows into the air between the smoker's puffs. Mainstream smoke is the smoke exhaled by the smoker. Smokers are only endangered by the smoke they directly inhale from tobacco, but people exposed to secondhand smoke breathe in both sidestream and mainstream smoke.

In one study on passive smoking, a group of about 32,000 women were followed over a ten-year period. None of these women smoked, but some were regularly exposed to second-hand smoke at their homes or jobs. The women exposed to smoke were found to be twice as likely to have heart attacks. Scientists further estimate that secondhand smoke causes more than 3,000 lung cancer deaths and 37,000 heart disease deaths each year among nonsmokers.

Smoke from other people's cigarettes can be hazardous to your health.

Children are especially vulnerable to the effects of second-hand smoke. This is because their developing tissues are more readily damaged. Children exposed to secondhand smoke for several hours each day visit hospital emergency rooms more often for breathing difficulties than children who are not

exposed. The children with secondhand smoke exposure are also more frequently hospitalized for respiratory breathing problems than unexposed children. According to the National Institutes of Health, children who breathe in secondhand smoke are at risk for a number of other health concerns. They are more likely to experience middle ear problems, coughing and wheezing, and worsened asthma conditions.

Many nonsmokers feel that they are sometimes forced to smoke against their will. Some have paid a very high price. Fifty-three thousand people die each year because of second-hand smoke.

Stores require people to show identification when buying tobacco products. At this store, a sign on the counter tells customers to have a photo ID, such as a driver's license or passport ready. The use of photo IDs is intended to prevent sales of cigarettes and other tobacco products to minors.

Chapter Three

Cigarettes and Youth

All fifty states have laws restricting tobacco sales to minors, but, unfortunately, many young people still smoke. The American Heart Association estimates that more than 3 million teenagers between the ages of twelve and seventeen are smokers.

For example, a young woman named Amanda was drawn in by the supposed glamour of smoking. A talented teenager with a bright future in dance and choreography, Amanda began smoking when

One study showed that young people who had at least three friends who were regular smokers were twenty-four times more likely to become regular smokers themselves.

her school dance troupe went on a two-month European tour. "My best friend was on the trip with me," Amanda recalled. "She was five-foot-ten, thin, and slinky and glamorous. And she smoked. I wanted to emulate her." Even before the tour was over, Amanda was hooked on cigarettes. She continued smoking cigarettes after the dance troupe returned.

Studies show that by the time they graduate from high school, one third of America's teenagers have smoked occasionally, while nearly one out of five smoke frequently. More than a third of young people who ever try smoking a cigarette become regular daily smokers before leaving high school. Among high school dropouts, the number of smokers skyrockets to 70 percent.

Serious Consequences

Underage smoking is often the start of a dangerous cycle. The vast majority of adult smokers began smoking before they were eighteen years old. In addition, studies show that young people are extremely likely to continue smoking once they've started.

Among young smokers, nicotine addiction can begin within days. As Dr. Joseph DiFranza, a professor of family medicine and community health at the University of Massachusetts School of Medicine, described it: "What we found is that kids are getting addicted to nicotine far more quickly than we ever thought possible. We have a lot of kids who start smoking when they're eleven or twelve years old, and they're addicted within a few weeks."

Amazingly, only a small amount of nicotine is needed for young people to get hooked. DiFranza continued, "We were surprised to find that the children were experiencing the same symptoms of nicotine addiction as adults who smoked heavily—even those kids who only smoked a few cigarettes a week . . ."

Underage smokers face all the health risks adult smokers do in addition to other risks associated with their youth. Smoking is particularly harmful to growing and changing young bodies. The two hundred known poisons in cigarette smoke can affect normal development.

A joint study by the National Institute of Mental Health (NIMH) and the National Institute of Drug Abuse (NIDA)

Regular Users

The earlier people start to smoke, the more likely they are to become regular tobacco users.

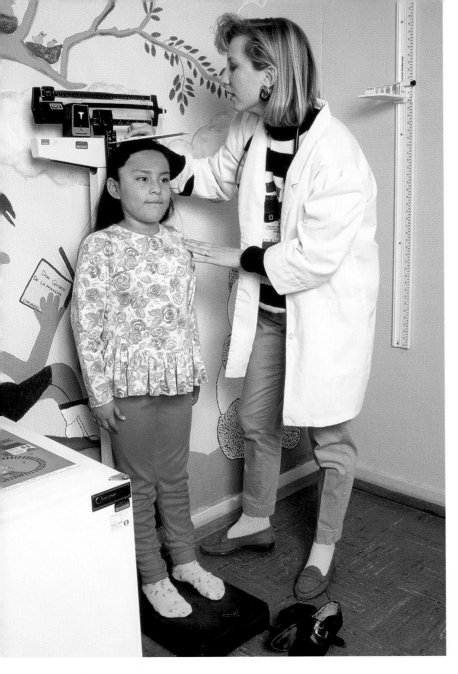

Smoking is especially harmful to children. It slows lung growth and reduces the oxygen available for muscles used in sports.

revealed that teens who smoke also have an increased risk of developing psychiatric disorders later on. These include panic attacks and agoraphobia. In a panic attack a person suddenly feels overwhelmed with fear for no apparent reason. The individual may experience rapid heartbeat, dizziness, sweating, trembling, and chest pains. Panic attacks, which occur without warning, can be extremely frightening.

Individuals with agoraphobia fear open spaces. They sometimes find it stressful to leave their homes. In commenting on the study, NIDA director Dr. Alan I. Leshner said, "This is important because it highlights how cigarette smoking may rapidly and negatively affect a teen's emotional health—perhaps even before any of the widely known physical effects such as cancer occur."

Why Young People Smoke

Young people smoke for a number of reasons. It sometimes has to do with the individual's home environment. Research shows that children from homes in which one or both parents smoke are more likely to smoke as well. The risk is even greater if an older brother or sister smokes.

Michelle, who at thirty-two now has emphysema, grew up in a smoker's household. She recalled: "I started smoking at the age of my youngest son, eight years old. My father smoked, my older sister smoked and I thought it was cool. Not so! Sadly, my father would die eight years later of emphysema. . . . My father started smoking at the age of seven, and died at the young age of fifty-nine leaving my disabled mother and me also two older sisters and one brother."

Teen rebelliousness has also been cited as a reason young people smoke. For some, smoking has the allure of a forbidden activity. Strong **antismoking** warnings by school officials and parents may only heighten its appeal for teens who defy authority.

In junior high and high school, social pressures influence some students to smoke. Young girls sometimes smoke to control their weight. They feel pressure to be thin and tobacco becomes their diet drug of choice. For them smoking cigarettes sometimes replaces meals.

Still larger numbers of teens smoke because their friends do. Eighty-one percent of the students who smoked at two vocational high schools in Virginia were found to have a best

Many young people feel pressured to smoke to fit in with their friends. While saying no can be difficult, your body will thank you.

friend who also smoked. Young people frequently have their first cigarette at a party or when they are out with their friends.

Lured by Advertising

Cigarette advertising can also entice young people to smoke. Despite denials by tobacco companies, cigarette manufacturers have been targeting the youth market through advertising

Undesirable Connections

Smokers are usually not the best students. Students who smoke earn fewer As and Bs than non-smokers. According to "Preventing Tobacco Use Among Young People: A Report of the Surgeon General," youthful smokers are more likely "to get into fights, carry weapons, [and] attempt **suicide** . . . "

over the years. The following is an excerpt from an internal memo at the R. J. Reynolds Tobacco Company entitled "Some Thoughts About New Brands of Cigarettes for the Youth Market":

> *... If our company is to survive and prosper. . . we must get our share of the youth market. . . Thus we need new brands designed to be particularly attractive to the young smoker. . . A new brand aimed at the young smoker must somehow become the "in" brand and its promotion should emphasize togetherness, belonging, and group acceptance, while at the same time emphasizing individuality and "doing one's own thing."*

For many years candy and bubble gum were sold in packages that looked like actual cigarette brands. Very small children used these to play at smoking, but some people saw this as a dangerous form of early training. In 1967 the Federal Trade Commission cited these products as "an indirect form of advertising aimed at children." The tobacco companies denied any such intent, and the products still remain available today.

In recent years the tobacco industry has effectively bypassed government bans on cigarette advertising by sponsoring sports and entertainment events. Among these are the Winston Cup Series and the Kool Jazz Concert. The tobacco industry's sponsoring of such events has not gone unnoticed by young people. In one survey more than half of the teens asked were able to name one such event and the brand of the sponsoring cigarette company. Researchers further noticed

Cigarette companies use sporting and entertainment events to promote their products.

that this type of event sponsorship tended to link cigarettes to a particular sport in the young person's mind.

Through another advertising method known as "brand stretching," cigarette manufacturers put cigarette logos on various products that are popular with teens. These may include backpacks, baseball caps, jackets, and sunglasses. A young person wearing one of these items is instantly turned into a walking advertisement for cigarettes.

Better Choices

By now, most young people have heard all of the reasons why they shouldn't smoke from health-care specialists. Still some teenage smokers refuse to listen to the warnings. Instead, they see themselves as invincible, thinking nothing will ever harm them. Yet sooner or later, many change their minds. Sometimes it's sooner than might be expected.

Though many of her friends smoked in high school, Jessica resisted the temptation to start. She explained what happened to some of her friends: "Most of my friends in high school started smoking to look older or more attractive. A few years later these same girls were trying every tooth whitener on the market to remove the tobacco stains. One even managed to take the enamel off her teeth. A big beige smile isn't very appealing. And getting cancer someday would be even less so."

Cigarette smoking has never made anyone more attractive, and the long-term effects of smoking are frightening. Eventually, all smokers face the more serious consequences of smoking, such as the higher risk of lung disease, heart disease, and stroke.

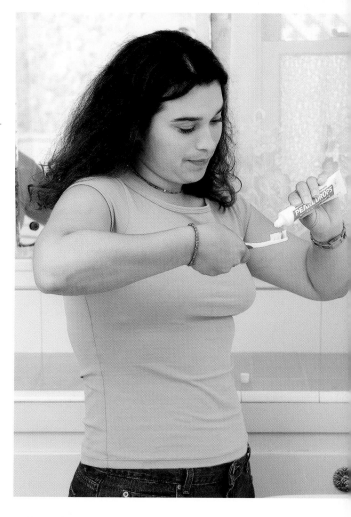

Smoking not only hurts your body, it hurts your appearance. It can stain your teeth yellow, and it causes wrinkles.

37

Former Surgeon General C. Everett Koop encourages people to stop smoking. This photograph was taken at a world conference on tobacco.

Chapter Four

Quitting

There are many good reasons to stop smoking. As former Surgeon General C. Everett Koop, M.D., once said, "If you have a spouse who's nagging you at home to quit, children who suggest that you're going to die if you don't, and then your boss says you can't smoke at the work site, that's a pretty good indication that it's time to quit."

After a while, the reason someone started smoking no longer matters. The person becomes hooked— smoking is an addiction that can be hard to break. Yet many people manage to quit and there are lots of good reasons to do so. The American Lung Association cites a few below:

How Quitting Changes Your Body

Twenty minutes after quitting	Blood pressure decreases Pulse rate drops
Eight hours after quitting	Carbon monoxide level in the body drops to normal Oxygen level in the body increases to normal
Twenty-four hours after quitting	Chance of heart attack decreases
Forty-eight hours after quitting	Nerve endings start to regrow Ability to smell and taste is enhanced
One to nine months after quitting	Coughing, sinus congestion, fatigue, and shortness of breath decrease
One year after quitting	The risk for heart attack is cut to half of that of a smoker
Five to fifteen years after quitting	The risk of stroke is reduced to that of someone who has never smoked
Ten years after quitting	The risk of lung cancer drops to as little as one-half that of someone who has continued smoking

Ways to Quit

People stop smoking in different ways. Some try to do it cold turkey, which means that they just stop smoking. Ideally, the last cigarette they smoke is the last one they ever smoke.

Other people try a more gradual approach. They cut down on the number of cigarettes they smoke each day. The idea is to gradually reduce their need for nicotine until they are able to stop completely.

Regardless of the method used, addicted smokers may experience withdrawal symptoms. They may feel tired, irritable, restless, and unable to concentrate. Some complain of stomach problems or being unable to sleep. For many, smoking cigarettes was a habit they enjoyed for some time. One former smoker compared the craving for cigarettes to "the longing you feel for a lost love."

Usually it takes several tries before a smoker quits for good. Yet some smokers who stop say it wasn't as hard as they expected. That's how it was for Peggy M., who once smoked about one and a half packs of cigarettes a day.

A person can experience symptoms of withdrawal, such as having difficulty concentrating, after quitting smoking.

41

She described her experience this way: "I had such dread of stopping. I'd tell myself, 'I'm nervous. I have a lot of pressures. I'm not up to this.' It just seemed so overwhelming to tackle. But once I tried it, it was not what I had built it up to be in my mind."

Tools to Help Quit

Often times, people need help to stop smoking. Many organizations, such as the American Cancer Society and the American Lung Association, offer stop-smoking programs. Not-On-Tobacco, or N-O-T, is a total-health approach to help teens quit smoking designed by the American Lung Association. In ten one-hour group sessions, young people learn daily life management skills as well as healthy lifestyle behaviors, such as proper nutrition and exercise. Specially trained facilitators who like teenagers and can treat them like adults run the groups.

The Food and Drug Administration has also approved several products to help smokers quit. These include nicotine

Kicking the Habit

Beth, a seventeen-year-old who gave up smoking, described what it was like for her to quit her cigarette habit this way: "I didn't think it would be hard to stop smoking, but it was. I would stop buying cigarettes then I would turn my house upside down looking for half smoked ones. Sometimes I felt like giving up but I couldn't. I turned this thing into a battle between me and cigarettes. I was determined to win and I finally did."

gum, patches, inhalers, and nasal sprays. The idea behind these products is nicotine replacement therapy. Nicotine is supplied to the person in a form other than a cigarette. This helps to reduce the symptoms of nicotine withdrawal until the person is weaned from tobacco.

Smokers trying to quit may also try a pill designed for this purpose. This pill does not contain nicotine. Instead, it affects the person's brain chemistry to reduce cigarette **cravings**.

Both nicotine replacement therapy and a pill to reduce nicotine cravings can be helpful. However, these aids tend to work best when used with a program that teaches behavioral changes. Such techniques assist smokers in avoiding cigarettes.

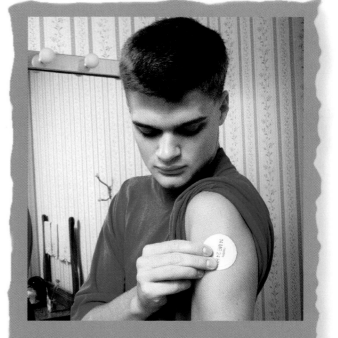

The Patch Approach

With a skin patch, nicotine enters the body automatically. Depending on the type of patch, the individual receives nicotine either over a twenty-four-hour period or only while awake. The patches come in different dosages, depending on the amount of nicotine needed by the patient.

The smoker also has to be firmly committed to the task at hand. As a respiratory therapist who conducts stop-smoking classes stressed, "A person's motivation cannot be underestimated. You have to really want to stop. [A] pill, the patch, gum—none of that is really going to help unless you really want to quit because nothing is going to completely erase the craving."

Perhaps the most important commentary about smoking

A group of people attend a stop-smoking class. Some people find that joining a stop-smoking program provides them with the necessary support to break the habit.

and quitting came from former Surgeon General C. Everett Koop, who said, "Quitting smoking is never as good as not starting to smoke." In the end, the best treatment for nicotine addiction may be prevention.

Tips to Quit Smoking

There are many things that you can do to help yourself break the cigarette habit for good:

- Exercise regularly. This helps to relieve tension and take your mind off smoking.
- Pick a specific day to stop smoking. Mark it on your calendar. Think of it as the first day of the rest of your life—a longer life.
- Think before you smoke. Instead of having a cigarette, try having a glass of water or a stick of gum.
- If you have a friend who's a smoker, try quitting together.
- Eat regularly. Sometimes hunger can be mistaken for cigarette craving.
- Keep the money you formerly spent on cigarettes in a special place. Once you're cigarette-free buy yourself a treat.
- Get enough sleep. Use relaxation techniques instead of cigarettes to relax.
- If you slip, don't give up. Keep trying—eventually you'll succeed.

These days, more and more places are deciding to prohibit smoking. Many forms of transportation, such as trains and airplanes, do not allow travelers to smoke on board.

No Smoking Permitted on This Side of Sign

No Smoking

Chapter Five

Changing Times

If smoking was once considered fashionable, times have certainly changed. In recent years steps have been taken to both curb smokers and limit the effects of secondhand smoke. Smoking is now prohibited at most job sites. It is also banned in public buildings, airports, and many restaurants. The movement to stop smoking is international. Similar steps have been taken in numerous European countries. In Japan you can even buy clothing made out of a smoke-repellant fabric.

Tobacco Industry Settlements

In an effort to challenge the tobacco industry, a host of lawsuits have been filed over the years. The largest of these resulted in a November 1998 agreement known as the Master Settlement Agreement. This settlement was signed by the major tobacco companies and the attorneys general in forty-six states and five U.S. territories. Under the agreement the tobacco industry promised to do the following:

- To pay $206 billion over twenty-five years to the forty-six states and five territories that signed.

The executives of five tobacco companies stand before the House Commerce Committee in Washington, D.C., in 1998.

- To remove billboard cigarette advertisements as well as advertisements in sports arenas.
- To stop using cartoon characters to sell cigarettes.
- To stop marketing cigarettes to young people.

Teens Against Smoking

Young people across America have been part of the anti-smoking movement. In Florida a group of teens was allotted a sizable sum from the state to start their own antismoking campaign. Choosing the name Truth for themselves, the teens' motto was: "Their brand is lies. Our brand is truth." These young people started Students Working Against Tobacco (SWAT) Clubs and attended Teen Tobacco Summits. They also developed some highly effective anti-smoking ads and TV commercials. As one seventeen-year-old high school junior described their work: "It's teens talking to teens—we're not telling them what to do. We're just letting them know what tobacco companies are doing to them."

A group of teenagers in Georgia is also making a difference in the campaign to end teen smoking in Georgia. They worked as "undercover agents" for the Chatham County Youth Commission in a study on tobacco and young people. The teens went to stores, restaurants, bowling alleys, and other places to see if these establishments sold cigarettes to minors. In many cases they found that they could have made the purchase. The study results were revealed by the Youth Commission at both a press conference and a county

Members of Truth, the antismoking group, remove cigarette advertisements from a banner made for an antismoking rally. The ads were sent back to tobacco companies as a protest against advertisements aimed at teenagers.

commission meeting. By exposing the easy access teens have to cigarettes, the young undercover agents hope that laws against selling tobacco to minors will be more strictly enforced.

Another sign of the changing times is an event called the Great American Smokeout. Sponsored by the American Cancer Society, the smokeout is held every year on the third Thursday of November. On that day smokers throughout the country give up cigarettes for twenty-four hours. Hopefully this is the start of kicking the habit for good. People of all ages are encouraged to take part. Weeks before, some high schools hold pep rallies. Local sports heroes urge young people not to start smoking or to quit if they've already started.

More to Be Done

Undeniably, change is under way. But the tobacco industry still advertises heavily. In 1999, the year following the Master Settlement Agreement, the industry increased its advertising spending to $8.4 billion dollars, or a million dollars an hour.

More Money Please

State officials had promised to spend most of the Master Settlement money on smoking prevention efforts. Yet, too often, such funding has gone for tax cuts, highway repairs, and other needs unrelated to smoking.

As Randolph Smoak, president of the American Medical Association, noted: "Every dollar that gets diverted away from tobacco prevention and cessation programs . . . is a win for the [tobacco] industry."

While cigarette manufacturers no longer use outdoor billboards, they have found other ways to promote their product. These include placing additional ads in magazines, designing more elaborate store displays, sponsoring exceedingly popular entertainment and sporting events, and even using the Internet.

Those in health care argue that more needs to be done because too many people are still smoking and dying. Health officials urge us all to fight back. A good way to start is by not smoking.

Timeline

1 B.C.	Native peoples in North and South America smoke tobacco.
1492	Columbus arrives in America. He is among the first explorers who bring tobacco back to Europe.
1607	The Jamestown Colony is founded. Tobacco plays an important role in its economy. This would be true for other southern colonies as well.
1861–1865	During the Civil War cigarettes become more widely used.
1881	The first cigarette-making machine is invented.
1914–1918	World War I brings a boost in cigarette sales.
1930s–1950s	Medical studies begin to link cigarettes to serious medical concerns.
1964	A government document known as the "1964 Surgeon General's Report on Smoking and Health" is released, citing smoking as a major cause of lung cancer. The report links cigarettes to other health concerns as well.
1966	The Federal Trade Commission requires that cigarette packaging and advertising carry health warnings.
1977	The first Great American Smokeout is held. This will become a yearly event.
1998	The Master Settlement Agreement is signed. The tobacco industry agrees to pay forty-six states and five U.S. territories $206 billion over twenty-five years.
1999	Teens help with the Chatham County Youth Commission's study on tobacco use among young people.
2001	The tobacco industry continues to spend more than $8 billion a year on advertising.

Glossary

addictive—something that causes the body to become dependent on it

antismoking—against smoking

carbon monoxide—a poisonous gas

craving—an extremely strong need or desire

emphysema—a serious lung disease that makes breathing difficult

lethal—deadly

mainstream smoke—smoke exhaled by a smoker

melancholia—depression

nicotine—a poisonous substance found in tobacco leaves

passive smoking—inhaling smoke given off by smokers

pesticide—a chemical used to kill insects

respiratory—having to do with breathing

secondhand smoke—the smoke given off by people smoking cigarettes and cigars. Also called environmental tobacco smoke.

sidestream smoke—the smoke from the lit end of the cigarette that never passes through a filter

suicide—taking one's own life

To Find Out More

Books

DeAngelis, Gina. *Nicotine & Cigarettes*. Philadelphia, PA: Chelsea House, 2000.

Haughton, Emma. *A Right To Smoke*. Danbury, CT: Franklin Watts, 1997.

Hirschfelder, Arlene B. *Kick Butts: A Kid's Action Guide To A Tobacco-Free America*. Parsippany, NJ: Julian Messner, 1998.

Hyde, Margaret O. *Know About Smoking*. New York: Walker, 1995.

Monroe, Judy. *Nicotine*. Berkley Heights, NJ: Enslow, 1995.

Pringle, Laurence P. *Smoking: A Risky Business*. New York: Morrow Junior Books, 1996.

Organizations and Online Sites

American Cancer Society
1599 Clifton Road N.E.
Atlanta, GA 30329
http://www.cancer.org
This community-based health organization is dedicated to preventing cancer and to helping those who have cancer.

American Lung Association
61 Broadway, 6th Floor
New York, NY 10006
http://www.lungusa.org
This organization was created to prevent lung diseases and promote lung health. Its online site offers information on the health effects of smoking.

Kickbutt
http://www.kickbutt.org
This online site contains information on how citizens can challenge tobacco industry wrongdoings. There's a special section on youth advocacy and activism.

National Center for Tobacco-Free Kids
http://www.tobacco-freekids.org
This online site will provide the latest news on smoking and youth, and it offers information on ways you can get involved.

Stop Teenage Addiction to Smoking (STATS)
Northeastern University
360 Huntington Avenue
241 Cushing Hall
Boston, MA 02115

Tobacco Information and Prevention Source
http://www.dcc.gov/tobacco
This government online site contains a TIPS 4 YOUTH section with smoke-free messages from famous people.

The Truth
http://www.thetruth.com
This organization's online site provides information about deceptive advertising practices as well as advice on how to quit.

A Note On Sources

There are numerous books, periodicals, and Internet sources available to writers researching tobacco use. Among the books I relied on were Richard Kluger's *Ashes to Ashes*, Joseph C. Robert's *The Story of Tobacco in America*, and Tara Parker Pope's *Cigarettes: Anatomy of an Industry from Seed to Smoke*.

Many of the quotes from smokers come from the book *The Last Puff* by John W. Farquhar, M.D., and Gene A. Spiller, Ph.D., the online sites About.com Smoking Cessation and News-Journal Online, as well as the American Cancer Society booklet *Smart Move! A Stop Smoking Guide*.

Pamphlets and reports that were especially helpful included several from the National Institute of Health, the U.S. Surgeon General's Office, the American Lung Association, and the American Cancer Society. Further data was gathered from such magazines, newspapers, and online sites as *The Detroit News*, *Patient Care*, *USA Today*, and CNN.com.

Besides using these sources, I spoke with many smokers to learn about their experiences. Some had recently stopped smoking, others were trying to stop, and several had lost family members because of tobacco-related illnesses. I appreciate their help and wish them only the best for the future.

—Elaine Landau

Index

Numbers in *italics* indicate illustrations.

About the Author

Popular author Elaine Landau worked as a newspaper reporter, editor, and as a youth services librarian before becoming a full-time writer. She has written more than two hundred nonfiction books for young people. She has written many books for Franklin Watts are on health topics, including *Autism*, *Tourette Syndrome*, and *Parkinson's Disease*. Ms. Landau, who has a bachelor's degree in English and journalism from New York University and a master's degree in library and information science from Pratt Institute, lives in Florida.